HOW TO TAPE
INSTANT ORAL BIOGRAPHIES

How to tape record, video or film your life stories.

by William Zimm

An easy-to-read large type book

This book belongs to

_____
name

_____
address

_____
phone number

Important family dates, birthdays, anniversaries, events, addresses, phone numbers and other information.

_____

_____

_____

_____

_____

_____

_____

_____

_____

_____

Trace your family's roots from the old country through Ellis Island to today. Create a family library of spoken histories. Sit down with someone you love or admire; flip on the tape recorder and tape their life stories and memories. You'll be able to hear their voices for ever.

Here is what people say about **How to Tape Instant Oral Biographies:**

"Mr. Zimmerman has an equation: Grandchild plus grandparent plus tape recorder equals 'living history.' It worked on Grandparents Day." **- The New York Times**

"A novel booklet, Instant Oral Biographies, gives... questions to prod even the most reticent interviewee into telling a full, rich story." **- Business Week**

"A young biographer will see himself in a new light when he researches and tapes his family's history." **- Parents Magazine**

"Designed originally to help youngsters draw out information from their parents and grandparents, it is also intended to spark one's own memory for oral autobiography." **- Publishers Weekly**

"Zimmerman's reporter's notebook not only makes oral biography easy, but turns it into a game that both parties can enjoy.... I wouldn't be surprised if his little guide...did as much to re-establish that old-fashioned family feeling as a week-long reunion." **- Jack Smith, Time of Your Life**

"Mr. Zimmerman has found that when children 'interview' their grandparents on tape, they produce a unique and treasured family document." **- Sesame Street Parents' Newsletter**

*Bill Zimmerman and his daughter, Carlota,
interview Pastora Arena Garcia, grandmother.
Looking at old photos sparks memories.*

HOW TO TAPE

INSTANT ORAL BIOGRAPHIES

How to tape record, video or film your life stories.

by William Zimmerman

A Guarionex Press Book
(Say Gwah-ree-oh-nex)
New York

*For my wife, Teodorina, for her love,
and for my mother, for her encouragement.*

HOW TO TAPE INSTANT ORAL BIOGRAPHIES

Other books by William Zimmerman:
A BOOK OF QUESTIONS
to keep thoughts and feelings
MAKE BELIEFS:
A Gift Book for your Imagination
LIFELINES:
A Book of Hope

Front and back cover illustrations by Tom Bloom

CONTENTS

The author's maternal grandparents, Ida and Louis Edelbaum, and his mother, Ruth, as a baby. Today's technology preserves yesterday's history.

Preface

A sense of family has always been important in my life. Family has been the source of strength to me as well as much pain.

Much of my early adult years was spent in breaking away from my people, searching for my dead father, rebelling against family closeness.

I tried to establish a new family made up only of people I had chosen to be its members.

I chose a career in journalism as a way to broaden my life and found after interviewing hundreds of strangers I was better able to know myself. I learned that many of my fears, my dreams were shared by others.

The years passed. I am now father of a young daughter and have reached the same age my parents were when they had young children. I judge them less now. I can appreciate their struggles and understand more clearly why they were the way they were.

I wrote this book—sort of a how-to-do-it guide for recording one's family history—to help me understand better my parent's lives and hence my own.

I wrote it to help preserve for myself, my daughter and perhaps for generations to come something of the voice of my family that is very special. I wrote it to draw us all closer and give each of us a chance to record and appreciate our stories.

WEZ

"Abuela, tell me about when you were growing up."

Everyone has a story to tell

*-If only someone would listen,
If only someone would ask.*

*"Now here's the cassette with the story
Grandmother Ruth told me about how Papa
raised chickens in his bedroom when he was little"*

WHAT'S
AN _INSTANT_ ORAL BIOGRAPHY?

Grandma, what were you like as a little girl?

Dad, how'd you meet mom? What was she like then?

Cindy, what was the turning point of your life?

Aunt Ann, what was I like when I was little?

Remember asking the questions? Remember the stories you heard? Wouldn't you give much of what you own today if you could hear the voice or advice of an honored ancestor or special relative who is no longer around?

Every person has a story, a biography, a family history worth telling and saving—not only famous people.

But not everyone knows how to record it quickly and easily or in a form that is organized and can be preserved.

This book presents a method to help you become an instant biographer or reporter and save the stories of your family and friends. It encourages you to capture the special voices and stories of the people you love and respect while they are still alive, their memories still sharp in their minds.

The *Instant Oral Biographies* concept proposes that with the use of tape recorders, recording or home video tape systems, and simple interviewing techniques, *anyone* — child or adult — can easily prepare oral biographies to track their families' chronicles and development much in the same way we traditionally have used cameras and home movies for this purpose.

Only, instead of film cameras alone, we also can use audio and video tape recorders — the tools journalists use to conduct interviews and preserve large amounts of information.

The objective of *Instant Oral Biographies* is to help you create a family library of spoken histories which you and future generations can listen to, both to understand the people in your families better and help you answer some of the questions you have about your background.

Such recordings, in helping us learn more about our families and our friends, also enable us to know more about ourselves. These are the people who influenced our own lives and caused us in part to be the way we are.

The guides in this book apply interviewing techniques I have learned and developed over the past 20 years as a professional journalist. I have interviewed thousands of people for their stories — from the chief executives of the world's largest banks to the person in the street looking for work.

They incorporate teaching techniques I also have used as managing editor of a daily national newspaper to train numerous inexperienced people to become, in time, outstanding journalists in their field.

This book presents instructions to teach you how to interview relatives and friends; a comprehensive list of suggested questions to ask in recording family biographies, and family history sheets which you can fill in as you interview or later on. The sheets have been duplicated to allow at least two people in a family to fill them in.

You are encouraged to add your own questions; space has been left at the end of the questions section to write them down or make notes of what you learn during the interview.

The section on suggested questions was designed to answer what is perhaps the most difficult problem any interviewer faces — sustaining a conversation with someone by asking readily understood, provocative questions that elicit meaningful and interesting answers.

The questions in this book include both straight-forward ones to get short, factual responses in some chronological order — important to any biography — and more open-ended questions to encourage people to open up and give broader responses.

I also believe that with the use of the suggested questions anyone can interview him or herself and make an autobiographical tape.

A parent, for example, could make such a recording to send to his or her child on a special occasion, such as a birthday or anniversary.

Similarly, the oral biographies can provide you with a means to hand down to your family and friends special messages, advice or testaments that complement the written letters and legacies you wish to leave to others.

Taping one's own history could also provide a very beneficial experience to, say, a relative who is often alone or bedridden and would like to take on a useful activity.

They also provide the visually handicapped with an easy method to record their stories.

In putting together these oral biography guidelines, I hold the basic premise that there is value in all people, that each of us has something to say that is worth telling others and remembering.

More of us would also believe this if we could be encouraged to talk more and answer questions, such as the ones posed in this book.

There is no doubt we enjoy sitting together and trading memories with one another; most of us like to hear about other peoples' lives to see how they coped with the basic life processes — making a living, raising a family, finding the strength to overcome personal crises.

We all like to compare notes.

The oral interviewing techniques I am proposing here will give everyone a chance to tell his story with help from you as the interested family member or friend, the "instant reporter."

Think of the wonderful possibilities of putting together such oral biographies:

■ They provide a means by which a family can be drawn together in a more meaningful way to record and listen to the stories of grandparents, parents, aunts, uncles and children. What better way for a grandchild to learn the stories of his grandfather and appreciate the special richness of our distinct backgrounds?

■ They enhance the happiness and poignancy of our meetings, especially such family occasions as a parent's birthday, anniversary, Mothers, Fathers or Grandparents Days, religious holidays and vacations.

■ They make people feel better about themselves. Richness is given—by those telling the stories of their lives and by those who ask and give others the chance to share and *save* their histories.

■ They preserve our special voices at a time when the world and its values are changing so rapidly and when individual family members are scattering around the earth.

■ They help us in our quest to reach back and trace our history, and support our belief that our traditions are worth preserving.

■ Oral biographies help elderly people break their silences by making them feel they are being heard. They can be used by those who work with the aged to help them capture the stories and advice they might want to leave to family and friends.

■ The interviews for oral biographies can be used in schools and colleges to develop students' listening and verbal skills and their understanding of history. The guides here can help them ask questions, recall answers and teach them something of the process of journalism and historical research.

The interviews can help young people realize, as do journalists, that there is much to learn from other people and that we each have a history which has value. Students should be encouraged to hear one another's tapes in order to share their heritages.

■ The interviews can be used to good effect as a way to draw people out of their problems by specialists who provide social, religious, health, educational and counseling services.

■ The interview techniques suggested here can also be applied by all of us in our daily lives to gain information and make our interactions with others, including strangers, easier and more meaningful.

They also can be employed at times of mourning when people gather together to capture memories of the dead people we loved. Taping the stores we have about this person can be a way to deal with our grief.

There also are unexpected benefits in making oral biographies. In my own case, after making a biographical tape of my mother, I'm still not sure who got more satisfaction and good feeling from the experience, she or I.

She felt better for having shared some of her life with me and said she had wanted to say some of the things we discussed long before the taping, but had not had the occasion previously to do so.

The interviewing, she said, gave her a certain emotional release which she felt positive about and gave us both a constructive way to explore the past together in order to meet and come to closer terms with one another.

I felt better for having a deeper understanding of why certain things were the way they were.

I listen to the tapes from time to time and I am proud to have them and share with my wife and daughter.

I will always be able to hear my mother's voice.

Three generations together— author's wife, Teodorina Bello de Zimmerman, with daughter, Carlota, and Pastora Arena.

*Over a cup of coffee, the author tapes the stories
his mother-in-law, Pastora Arena Garcia, tells
about her childhood in Puerto Rico.*

HOW TO INTERVIEW PEOPLE

1. An interview is a way for you to talk with someone with the help of questions for the purpose of obtaining information. ■

In the case of making an *Instant Oral Biography,* you are trying to record parts of someone's life story.

Keep in mind what all journalists do when asking questions — every fact has several parts to it that answer the questions of who? what? where? when? why? and how?

2. The best interviews occur when both the interviewer and the person being questioned have had time to prepare a little and think about what they want to accomplish through the interview. ■

Before you actually begin an interview it is important that you explain what your purpose is in compiling this oral biography.

You might say, for example:

"Mama, I'd like to hear your story, what your parents were like, what your earliest memories are, what life was like when you grew up. I'd like you to tell me and my children what your beliefs are. I will be using the tape recorder when you speak in order to make a living record of you as well as other members of our family that we can have for always and which future generations can hear."

As you say this, in fact, you might even want to test the recorder, tape what you are saying, and then play it back to the person being interviewed. It is a way to begin and to show the other person how the recording process takes place. It can overcome their fear of making the tapes.

Also, in calling your relatives or friends for an appointment for the interview, you might ask them to gather some old pictures of their parents and family members as well as documents such as passports, citizenship papers or marriage certificates you can review together.

Looking at old pictures with someone can often help people remember stories or past experiences which will be wonderful to have as part of the oral biography. Read letters aloud.

You might even want to bring with you an atlas to see where your relatives lived before they came to this country. A paperback, such as the Rand McNally *Historical Atlas of the World*, is an excellent vehicle to trace some of the older countries which have since been absorbed by larger nations.

3. Try to overcome your own fears of handling a tape recorder, which will be playing all the while you are interviewing. ∎

The machine should be looked upon as an aid, a friend if you will, just as it is the companion of thousands of journalists.

So before you begin interviewing, try it out, practice with it, fool around with it, make mistakes with it. And you will see that with practice, it works for you, not against you. It is much easier to record than to write down answers.

If you do not own a tape recorder or recording system, you can rent them. Look in the *Yellow Pages* phone directory under the subject listing: *Recorders, Sound—Equipment & Supplies.*

Bring along to the interview extra batteries, if you use them for your recorder, and extra tapes. Make sure the tapes are of the best quality sold because you want them to last for many, many years.

Also take with you a pen or pencil in case you want to make some notes to yourself on the special pages set aside in this book as you go along in the interview.

4. Think of an interview as having a conversation with someone in which you are asking most of the questions to keep the talk going and to keep it interesting.■

To have a good talk, try to conduct the interview in a quiet place where there are just the two of you so that some intimacy is achieved and thoughtful answers obtained.

You might want to do the interview in a kitchen or living room in which both of you are seated comfortably. Have a cup of coffee or tea together as you talk.

Later, as the interviewing process progresses well, it is possible that you might want to have other family members or friends around to join in and add to the responses.

5. Try to reassure the person being interviewed■

Some peoples' initial reactions to a request to do an oral biography might be to say that they have nothing important to tell you. But you know better. It is important you get across the message that you believe what they have to say has value.

Try to convey to them that the answers and thoughts they present are important for they will help serve as a family's record of its history, its survival, and you are trying to preserve their voice.

When people tell you, "I have nothing important to say," they really are saying, "Encourage me, help me see my life has meaning."

6. At first the people you will interview might naturally be somewhat nervous or apprehensive but this should not be surprising because most people have never been interviewed before. ■

You might even find, as I have, that until the people you interview get comfortable they will tend to lead the conversation where they want and perhaps not give you the types of responses you want.

But, don't worry about letting people wander a little in giving their answers. That's how you get interesting information. Just make a note in the book about what point you want to go back to, and return to it later.

Don't feel you have to be in total control over the interview all the while. It takes away the fun. The best interviewers regain control in a quiet way by coming back later to the questions that interest them.

7. The most effective interviewers also give as much as they take.■

This means they listen as carefully as possible to what a person is saying — or not saying.

Listening well is important; if you hear an answer that is interesting, you can be ready to encourage the person to elaborate further. It is important to convey to the person you are interviewing that you really want to hear their point of view.

I have found from my own experience in asking questions that people often don't come outright with clear answers. They may offer instead cues or phrases or start a sentence they don't finish. Listen carefully, then, for this may be someone's way of signaling you to ask them more about what they meant to say.

8. A good interviewer brings out the best in his or her subject and is often a prompter of inner thoughts.■

You might offer an example from your own experience to help someone being interviewed better understand the question you are asking.

Or, you might help them recall an answer by starting the question with a story you remember, such as:

"Remember, dad, the time we went fishing with Uncle Ed and he fell into the water and..."

Help the other person remember, but be patient while they think through what you are asking.

9. The interview you are conducting is to get the other person's story, not yours, even though the other person may tell you a lot about yourself.■

You may very well know the answers to some of the questions you ask, but for the purpose of compiling an oral record, you should let the person you are interviewing give the answers. And never cut them off.

10. Let me reassure you about asking questions■

Despite what your parents or your teachers may have told you when you were little, you shouldn't be afraid to ask questions of people.

I agree that it takes some courage and confidence to interview others; I, too, have felt fear and trepidation before interviewing strangers. But you will be interviewing family and friends.

The worst thing that can happen to you is that they will not want to answer a question or will laugh at you. But this is no skin off your back.

As do all journalists, you catch your breath and go on; you always can go back to a question later on if you do not initially get a completely satisfactory answer.

Remember, most interviewers ask the same questions many times during an interview until they get an answer they want. They just phrase the question differently each time they ask it.

Most times, however, people will answer your questions if you show you really are interested, and will give you wonderful answers.

11. In reviewing the suggested interview questions offered in this book, feel free to use only those that interest you the most.■

Change them if you want or add ones that you want; and, of course, improvise as you go along in the interview. If you are not asking questions you truly are interested in, then it is likely you will not get the effective responses you want to have for the recording.

Also, choose only those questions you feel comfortable with. There were some questions, for example, which I could not bring myself to ask of my mother when we were making our tape.

12. Study the questions offered in this book so that you are familiar with them. You might even want to practice saying them out loud in a quiet corner in your home so that you get used to them.■

You may also want to set particular goals beforehand as to what you hope to come away from the interview with. For instance, you might want to learn more about what you were like as a five-year-old and what was occurring in your other family members' lives at that particular point in time; or, you might want to gain new insight into a family problem that troubled you.

You may want to focus on finding out what life was like for that person when they were your age. What changes did each decade of growth bring?

You can show the subject the questions in this book before the interview to help them prepare their thoughts, but you do risk losing spontaneity of response.

13. By no means do you have to ask all the questions you have at one sitting.■

Interviewing can tire both you and the other person. You want to take pleasure in the process; so I suggest you do interviews of half-hour to one-hour duration over a number of sessions.

Having several or many interviews can do much to make visits with relatives — particularly with parents and grandparents — more meaningful. There then is something to be learned from each visit.

14. You are asking people to recount their life stories and you should remember that recalling different memories will arouse all kinds

of feelings and emotions in both you and the person being interviewed — tears, laughter, anger, joy, sadness can come. Respect these feelings; be understanding of the other person's feeling. Be gentle with them.■

I also would not worry about pauses, broken sentences, stutterings or any other verbal imperfections that are captured on the tape. After all, these reflect the way we speak and communicate — they are real — and my feeling is we should not edit them out.

During her recording my mother cried when she recalled something about her own mother which had touched her. We stopped for a moment — the tape still running — and then went on. She said later that she was glad to have remembered the event, for even with the pain, it helped her remember how she was as a little girl. For me, as I relisten to the recording, that moment of feeling is very precious.

15. After you finish conducting the interview, reassure the person that what they said was important to you.■

In answering your questions people are gifting you with a part of themselves and they may feel somewhat vulnerable after the experience; I have learned that interviewing can be a draining experience for both the person being interviewed and the one asking the questions.

You might want to call the person you interviewed the next day to thank them for helping you learn so much more about the people in your family and for the pleasure it gave you.

16. **Keep yourself as organized as possible, particularly when you are doing a series of interviews that will use many cassette tapes.** ■

Number each tape on its surface label; note what side tape it is; who was being interviewed; who was interviewing; the relationship between the two, such as mother and son; the date, and whether the interviewing was done on a special occasion, such as a birthday.

In fact, it is useful to start each tape with an introduction summarizing the above information. You might say, for example: "This is side two of the interview with my mother, Mary Jones, done on May 3, 1979. It is her 50th birthday. This is Bill Jones speaking."

Similarly, if you do another interview with the same person at a later date, you might state at the beginning of the tape that this interview is a continuation of an earlier one done on May 3, 1979.

In those instances where a tape runs out right in the middle of someone answering a question, I suggest you make a written note of where you were at so that when you change the tape you can add a sentence in the beginning to aid in the transition from one tape to another. You might say for example: "Mother, you were just talking about the time you took that trip to Europe. Please go on."

And to help you keep track of the content of each tape, consider attaching a summary sheet of the subjects covered and where they are found on the tape. Most tape recorders have a counter built into them for tracking tape footage. (As an example, your summary might note: mother's first love, 10-85.)

I further suggest you interview people one at a time, rather than in groups which are hard to control and where the noise level gets so high it is hard to keep track of who is saying what.

If you decide to interview during one of those rare occasions when people come from far away to gather at one place, such as a wedding, then consider drawing people away, one at a time, to a quiet room for a short interview.

And consider focusing the interviews on one theme or subject, such as their remembrances of the bride or groom when they were children or how they themselves felt on the day of their own marriage, or what advice they can offer the newlyweds.

Remember, the more you interview, the better a reporter you will become. The art of being a good interviewer is thinking about what you want to accomplish, asking clear questions, listening carefully and encouraging people to be confident that you respect what they have to say.

VIDEO, HOME-MOVIE IDEAS

What better use for a new home video or film system than to make a videotape or movie of your favorite people as you interview them about their lives, their memories, their traditions?

Where audio tapes, like radio, provide a certain mystery by making us imagine what people look like behind the voices we hear, video and film cameras perform the miracle of bringing the peoples' actual images to us.

Whether you decide to use video or film for all or portions of these interviews, or *Instant Oral Biographies,* as I call them, here are some ideas for using these media:

From time to time in the interview take pictures of the old family photographs, documents, maps, newspaper clippings or heirlooms the person refers to. Encourage people to bring with them their favorite family treasures collected over the years or handed down from generation to generation. You can focus the zoom camera on the photos as the person talks about them or even shoot them from behind the shoulder of the person holding them.

A woman being interviewed might want to show a traditional folk costume that her people wear on special national holidays, or even a wedding dress or shawl that was given to her by her mother.

If a family bible has been kept through the years and important events noted in it, why not have the person hold open its pages for you to record on videotape or film?

Similarly, a person may want to show a brooch or pair of earrings, or a favorite piece of china or glass figurine that was given to her by someone special or on a special occasion.

Think also of capturing a picture of the person near a special symbol that characterizes the family name or history. This might be a coat-of-arms, a book, a religious symbol such as a cross or Jewish mezuzah, or it could be a scarred old table, a porch swing, a cluttered attic, a grown tree planted when you were very young.

You might also want to videotape or film objects associated with the person whom you interview. These might be a cluttered desk, a typewriter, a knitting bag or sewing box, a fishing rod, a model ship.

How about a music stand or instrument, an old record, a loved pet, a favorite plant or brand of cigarettes, a home-made doll? An easel? In your home movie or video tape you may want to show the person handling or using such objects.

While you are most interested in focusing on the person's face, you may at other times want to zoom in on the eyes or mouth. Other times you may want to show, with the help of proper light, only a silhouette. If the person talks a lot using his hands, then why not focus on them? If someone talks of his marriage, why not zoom in on his wedding band?

You may also want to seat a child next to the person you interview to show two generations reaching out to one another. A child often helps draw out people's thoughts and feelings, and can conduct the interview while you tape them both.

Or, if the subject is seated in a favorite room why not pan the camera around the room as she talks about her life?

Here are other ideas for video or film: showing someone teaching how to cook or bake a family recipe, singing, making repairs, lighting candles for a holiday, telling stories to children while putting them to bed, reading a favorite poem or passage from a book, dancing, or even filming them listening to the exchange of marriage vows at a wedding or saying them at an anniversary party.

You might also want to film the person playing a record of a loved piece of music or poem and have them talk about the memories these evoke, or the meaning they hold in their life. Have them read aloud an old letter.

It is left to you decide if you, the interviewer, are to be on camera, too, while doing the questioning.

If so, a tripod can be used for this purpose to position the camera and keep it stationary. If you don't have a tripod, wedge the camera in between some books and prop the lens on some others to keep it stationary. Or, why not have another family member or close friend act as cameraperson, while you and your subject are engaged in the interview.

Sometimes the reactions of the interviewer to the stories being told can be as interesting and arresting as the faces of the person speaking. This is especially true in an interview where a son or daughter learns something new from questioning a parent.

If someone talks about her brother, you may want to focus the camera on a photograph of that person, or later film a short interview with the brother which could be edited with the tape or film to follow the first mention of him.

It also might be appropriate at the next family gathering to pan the camera or video recorder across the faces, one by one, of the people mentioned by your subject in her stories. And as you film them, identify them by name. This is particularly important if you are taping a reunion where many people gather. In reviewing an audio tape or video tape you might decide later to go out and shoot the places mentioned during the interview. For example, if someone tells you that he first lived in a small cold water flat when he came to this country, or on a small farm in another country, you may at some point want to visit the site and capture that location on film or tape.

I would encourage you to have the subject come with you when you do the shooting of these places so that he or she can convey to you first hand the feelings and impressions this reunion brings. The biography then takes on the character of an odyssey, one which each of us takes with our life.

If, however, you cannot physically go to a faraway location, consider having someone who lives there send you a photograph of the place which you can later put on tape.

A final reminder: Before you begin, show the subject how the equipment works as you test it so that he will not be afraid.

Also, because you are making a film where visual image is so important, it is not necessary to use sound throughout or have the subject talking constantly. Silent moments can add poignancy, drama and emotional depth to a tape as you show the subject simply sitting alone or perhaps playing with his or her grandchildren.

As with the oral biographies captured on audio tape, do not forget to record an introduction for each video cassette or film cartridge you use. This should include the subject's name, relation to you, your name, the date, location and occasion. This can be spoken by you or printed on cue cards that can be filmed or taped.

You can have some fun writing or drawing such introductions, such as coming up with a title like this:

Tuohy Family Productions
Presents
The Video Biography of
Grandma Celia Epstein

And how about using the family cat as the mascot for your home production?

If you like, you can involve other family members in producing the video or film biography: one person does the interviewing, another monitors sound, another makes the introduction and list of credits at the beginning of the tape and tells who did what.

By having other family members participate, you give them the opportunity to become familiar with your new equipment, to have fun, and most important, to make grandmother feel that everyone truly wants to know her life stories.

How can you lose?

These suggestions for videotaping or filming *Instant Oral Biographies* are offered with the intention of awakening your own ideas.

Taping an *Instant Biography* — whether on audio cassette, video or film—is a personal adventure between you and your subject. Approach your mission with a sense of care, sensitivity and art.

BEFORE YOU BEGIN . . .

Before beginning your interview, I suggest you do three things.

■ The first is to look over the questions in the next chapter several times, even a day or two before the interview; select and mark off the ones you like and change the ones you don't like. They are merely a tool to help you get started, and spacing has been left between each question for you to change them or add your own; there also are work pages at the end of the question section to add even others.

■ The second is to test your equipment and tape an introduction to the interview. You might begin this way:

"This is (state your name) speaking. Today (give month, date, year), I am interviewing (state full name of the person) who is my (give the person's relationship to you)."

If the interview is occurring on a special occasion, such as a birthday, then it would be

good to say what the occasion is.

■ The third thing to do is review the blank family history sheets in this book. As you conduct the interview—or even later on after it is over—you might want to fill in on the appropriate charts the names of the different people who were mentioned during the interview. The family charts have been duplicated to allow each marriage partner to have a set.

■ Finally, consider making duplicates of the tapes for your family.

With these duplicates, we can gift one another with tapes of our life stories and memories the same way we send letters and cards. We can offer them as presents at reunions.

Always buy the best quality tapes and enclose them in a storage container where they can be protected from dust or extremes of temperature. These tapes should be cared for with love because they are delicate and carry a treasure which you want to preserve. As an extra precaution, if you have the time and patience, consider transcribing them.

People sometimes tell me that they gave their parents a tape recorder for Christmas to record their memories but that no tapes were ever made. I tell them what their parents really want is for them to sit down with them and coax the memories out of them; they want interaction.

Now, with recorder, tapes and pen in hand, let's begin. On to the questions.

QUESTIONS TO ASK

What is your full name? (In interviewing a married woman ask for her maiden name as well.)

Do you know what your first name means or whom you were named after?

And did you personally know this person, and what were they like?

Does your family name have a special meaning?

Bill Zimmerman records his daughter's stories and jokes.

When were you born?

Where — at home, in a hospital, elsewhere? And in what city and country?

What is your nationality?

Was your family name changed when your family originally came to this country? What was it? In what language?

Who were the first family members to settle in this country? What were their names?

What brought them here and how did they get the money to come here?

Where did they first arrive? What possessions did they bring with them?

What language did they speak and where exactly did they come from? Did the place they came from have a different name from what it is called today?

Do you know any stories they might have told about what life was like for them before they came here?

Where did they first settle when they came here? How did they make their living?

Do you know when and where your grandparents were born? Their full names?

Do you remember any of the stories your grandparents would tell you about where they came from or what life was like for them when they were younger? What are some of these stories?

Do you know where they are buried?

What were the full names of your own parents?

When and where were they born and brought up?

What were your parents like?

How did they make a living?

Did you have many aunts or uncles? What were their names and what do you remember about them?

Who were your favorite relatives, and why?

Did you have any brothers or sisters? What were their names and when were they born in relationship to you?

What were they like as young people? Do you remember any special or funny stories about them?

Where did you live as a child, and what was your home town like back then? Can you describe your own home for me? What do you miss most about it?

Can you tell me what life was like when you were very young and growing up? What are some of your earliest memories?

What did you look like? What were you like as a young child? Serious? Always getting into trouble? Quiet? Sad? Happy? Can you think of any stories to show the way you were?

·Any funny ones?

Did you have a nick name? How did you get it?

How much schooling did you have? What was your favorite subject? What subject did you hate?

Did you have a favorite teacher and what was he or she like? How did they influence you?

Did you work as a child? What did you do?

What did you like doing most as a child? What games or instruments did you play? Did you have a favorite pet or toy?

Who were your best friends and what did you do together?

What is the happiest memory in your childhood and when did it happen?

What was the saddest time?

What was your first experience with death? What happened? What did it mean to you? How did you deal with the loss?

What beliefs or ideals do you think your parents tried to teach you to live your life?

Who do you think influenced your life the most when you were young, and in what way?

What great person have you known in your life? What made them special?

What were your teenage years like?

What goals did you have as a young person and what goals, if any, did your family have for you?

Did you go to college and what did you study?

What led you to choose the type of work you do or did? What is there about it you liked the most? the least?

When did you start working and what kinds of jobs were your first ones? What were they like and how did you do on them?

How much money did you make?

When did you first meet your (husband, wife)? Under what circumstances?

What was (he, she) like when you first met? What attracted you to (him, her)? Or did you dislike one another at first? Why?

How old were you both?

What was your courting like?

How soon after meeting did you marry?

What was life like in the early days of your marriage?

Where did you live? Was it hard to get by? How did you make your living? What was a typical day like for you at work or home?

Did you have any problems in the early years of your marriage? What about? What advice do you offer others for living together?

Did you go to war? Which one? Where were you stationed and what was it like? How long did you serve and in what branch?

When did you have children? (Ask for the names of the children and the dates each was born and the place.) What were your and your spouse's feelings during the pregnancy? Did anything unusual happen at birth?

Who was each child named after? (If children were adopted or came from other marriages, ask about the events surrounding these events.)

What were the children like? How did they differ from one another?

When you think back to the children when they were very young, what stories come to mind about them? How did the children change your life? How do you raise children to be good human beings?

What do you remember about me as a child? What was I like then? Whom do I take after? Was I very different from the way I am today?

What values did you try to impart to the children — religious, moral, social, other?

If a marriage partner has died, ask about when this occurred and how. Where are they buried?

If a divorce or separation occurred, ask about when this happened and the events that led to this. If there were other marriages, you might want to ask the person being interviewed about them — to whom were they married, when and where did the marriage occur, how did they meet and what children came from the union?

Looking back, what do you think has been the happiest time in your life? What was the worst? How do you get over sad periods? What helps you attain peace of spirit?

What do you think was the turning point in your life? How did your life change after this event? How did you learn to stand on your own two feet? When?

What have been the major accomplishments in your life?

What have been the biggest problems, mistakes or adversities in your life? And how did you overcome them or what did you learn from them? How did they affect your life?

If you were to give advice to me or my children today or even to the children to come in our family's future generations, what would it be? What have you learned from life? What has been its biggest surprise?

How do you think is the best way to conduct our lives?

What do you think your strengths are? What special things do you know that you are proud of?

What are your deepest values?

What makes you happy? Sad?

How do you overcome your fears?

What activities do you enjoy most — sports, cooking, reading, working, music, studying a certain subject, traveling? Others?

What is the most wonderful place you visited? What is your favorite time of year or holiday?

Is there a particular thought, or a saying, or a joke or a poem or song you would like to tell, read, recite or sing for me? I would love to hear it.

Is there a story that was told to you as a child which you would like to recall for me? What is it?

Tell me about an adventure you had. Your strangest experience? Your funniest?

Is there a family story, a prayer, an anecdote or saying you would like to have us remember always? What is it? Can you say it in another language?

Looking ahead, what things do you want to accomplish in life? What are your dreams?

If you had your life to do all over again, what would you do differently?

Are there any thoughts you'd like to add?

_____

Thank you for sharing these memories with me. I have learned much from you.

Here is space for you to note additional questions which you would like to ask or which have arisen while you were doing the interviews. Jot down any thoughts or impressions that come to mind as well as any explanatory family information you might want to remember.

For example, you might want to write down some expressions used in the tapes that might be in another language and translate them.

_____

My Questions and Notes

_____

_____

_____

_____

_____

_____

_____

_____

_____

_____

_____

_____

ROUNDING OUT THE BIOGRAPHY

Once you have asked most of the questions you want to ask of a particular person, such as your father or mother or respected friend, you should be encouraged to interview other relatives or close family friends for their reminiscences about the person you first interviewed.

This can help give you a fuller picture of the person, for we are seen differently by different people.

In doing this, I suggest you tape another introduction saying whom you are interviewing, the date, and what their relationship is to the person they are talking about and whether they bear any relationship to you. Also have them state how long they have known the other person.

In interviewing these family friends or other relatives, you might ask, for example:

How and when did you meet my (mother, father, aunt, uncle, etc.)?

What are your recollections of how my (mother, father) was when you first knew (her, him)?

Has (she, he) changed much in (her, his) ways from when you first knew (her, him)?

What were some of the adventures you shared together?

What were your happiest experiences together? Your saddest?

What is the funniest story you remember about my (mother, father)?

What do you think are my (mother's, father's) outstanding characteristics?

By the way, this process of gathering other peoples' impressions of someone can be used to good advantage in trying to capture a spoken portrait of someone who has just died. The tapes help us to remember.

The main goal you are trying to achieve in interviewing friends and relatives is to get their impressions of another person. It would be good to encourage them to give examples and anecdotes.

OTHER USES . . .

In making your *Instant Oral Biography* tape library, you also can add tape selections for the purpose of preserving important family and religious traditions. Here are examples:

How does our family prepare for and celebrate special holidays, such as: Christmas, Easter, Three Kings Day, Ramadan, Passover, Chanukah, your favorite holiday? What special foods do we eat? What traditions do we follow?

What is your recipe to prepare that wonderful (pudding, cake, name dish) you make for Thanksgiving or Christmas? How do you prepare (ham hocks, other dishes)?

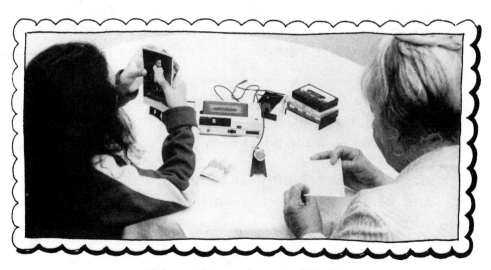

What shaped your life?

What ceremonies should we observe upon the birth of a boy child? A girl child? Twins?

What is the proper way to observe periods of mourning? What are our customs during and after a burial and the annual observance of a death?

What other rituals or customs do we follow for special occasions, such as birthdays, observing religious holidays, a period of engagement, the exchange of marriage vows?

What are your favorite family sayings? Who started them? Is there a way to say them in the language that was originally spoken in our family?

What are some of the home remedies our family has handed down generation to generation to treat certain ailments, such as a bad cold, upset stomach, rashes?

Tell me about some family superstitions. Or what things can I do to make my dreams come true or have good luck?

Are there any family diseases we suffer from and what are the symptoms we should watch for?

Are there special toasts we say in our family?

What are some good planting hints?

Are there other family traditions you would like us to keep alive? What are they?

The tapes can also provide us with a way to compile living records of each new generation's development.

For example, I have used the tape recorder to great advantage to make tapes of my daughter's first words and the stories she has told us. Interview your own children.

In interviewing my daughter, I want to know what makes her happy, sad or frightened. I want to understand her view of life, what she considers to be her best joke or most difficult riddle, her favorite or most hated person. What kinds of people does she like? What are some of her goals? What dreams does she remember? What nightmares? What wishes does she have? What advice can she offer me so that I can remember to enjoy life as openly as she? "Sing a song for me that you love," I ask her.

Even now, at the age of eight, Carlota enjoys listening to how she spoke or sang at a younger age. We have also used the recorder to tape some of her favorite stories which she can play when she is on trips away from home.

You might want to use the recorder to tape special events or ceremonies, such as the exchange of marriage vows, a Passover seder, a Bar or Bath Mitzvah, a religious service, a family prayer or important speech.

Use the interview technique to understand more clearly your own feelings and those of other people.

Those who are hospitalized for illness might consider taping their own feelings and experiences during treatment and recovery to help others who may go through the same sickness. These can be donated to a lending library at medical treatment centers.

Many communities, through their local libraries, historical societies or religious institutions, are using the oral history approach to compile an historical picture of their communities by interviewing local leaders and residents who have been around for some time.

Similarly, corporations can use this same approach to interview their senior executives who can trace the development of their enterprises over the years.

For children from divorced families where remarriages have occurred, the oral biographies approach provides a way for them to learn about and draw closer to their new relatives. And for newlyweds, taping interviews with new family members provides a rich way to learn about each other's backgrounds. Why not exchange tapes with your vows?

And for those about to go abroad to live or travel, why not consider taping oral biographies of family members who are close to you so that you can hear their voices when you are far away?

Interview yourself with the tape recorder to capture your impressions of what you see or learn during your exterior or interior journeys: what impresses you?, what frightens you?, what strikes you as funny?, what do you feel?

The tape recorder thus becomes your mechanical diary by which you hold onto and understand your thoughts and feelings. Sometimes, mail someone close to you such a cassette as you would a letter.

Remember, the approach you take to compiling *Instant Oral Biographies* should reflect your own interests and emphasize the type of information you personally want to preserve for generations to come as well as for yourself.

I hope you enjoy the process. I believe it can provide you with a wonderful way of finding your story and preserving the best parts of your life.

Teodorina, Carlota and Pastora Arena hear history at the kitchen table.

One side of the family

(Family's name)

The family history sheets that follow are not meant to be definitive; rather, they are to help you delineate in some organized form your family relationships.

Each of the tables has been duplicated in order to allow each partner in a relationship to use for outlining his or her own family organizations.

SPOUSE   ME

[(write full name) b. _____ d. _____]   married (date)   [(write full name) b. _____ d. _____]

MY CHILDREN AND GRANDCHILDREN

First born _____
     b. _____ d. _____
     Marriage date _____
     Spouse _____
     b. _____ d. _____
     Children:
     1. _____
     b. _____ d. _____
     2. _____
     b. _____ d. _____

Second born _____
     b. _____ d. _____
     Marriage date _____
     Spouse _____
     b. _____ d. _____
     Children:
     1. _____
     b. _____ d. _____
     2. _____
     b. _____ d. _____

Third born _____

    b. _____ d. _____

    Child's marriage date _____

    Child's spouse _____

    b. _____ d. _____

Third born's children:

    1. _____

       b. _____ d. _____

    2. _____

       b. _____ d. _____

Other personal or historical data which you may want to note. You can include educational accomplishments, trades and professions, other important dates, burial sites, remarriages, places of birth:

_____

_____

_____

_____

_____

_____

_____

_____

_____

_____

_____

_____

_____

_____

My other marriages:

    To whom _____

        b. _____ d. _____

    Marriage years _____

Children of marriage:

First born _____

        b. _____ d. _____

    Child's marriage date _____

    Child's spouse _____

        b. _____ d. _____

First born's children:

    1. _____

        b. _____ d. _____

    2. _____

        b. _____ d. _____

Second born _____

        b. _____ d. _____

    Child's marriage date _____

    Child's spouse _____

        b. _____ d. _____

Second born's children:

    1. _____

        b. _____ d. _____

    2. _____

        b. _____ d. _____

Other personal or historical data:

_____

_____

_____

_____

_____

_____

Spouse's other marriages:
   To whom _____
        b. _____ d. _____
   Marriage years _____
Children of marriage:
First born _____
        b. _____ d. _____
   Child's marriage date _____
   Child's spouse _____
        b. _____ d. _____
First born's children:
   1. _____
        b. _____ d. _____
   2. _____
        b. _____ d. _____
Second born _____
        b. _____ d. _____
   Child's marriage date _____
   Child's spouse _____
        b. _____ d. _____
Second born's children:
   1. _____
        b. _____ d. _____
   2. _____
        b. _____ d. _____

Other personal or historical data:

_____

_____

_____

_____

_____

_____

MOTHER   FATHER

married
(date)

_____
(maiden name)

b._____
d._____

_____
(name)

b._____
d._____

ME, MY BROTHERS AND SISTERS

First born _____

    b. _____ d. _____

Marriage date _____

Spouse _____

    b. _____ d. _____

Children:

  1. _____

    b. _____ d. _____

  2. _____

    b. _____ d. _____

Second born _____

    b. _____ d. _____

Marriage date _____

Spouse _____

    b. _____ d. _____

Children:

  1. _____

    b. _____ d. _____

  2. _____

    b. _____ d. _____

Third born _____

     b._____ d. _____

Marriage date _____

Spouse _____

     b. _____ d. _____

Children:

1. _____

     b._____ d. _____

2. _____

     b._____ d. _____

Fourth born _____

     b. _____ d. _____

Marriage date _____

Spouse _____

     b._____ d. _____

Children:

1. _____

     b._____ d. _____

2. _____

     b. _____ d. _____

Other personal or historical data:

_____

_____

_____

_____

_____

_____

_____

_____

_____

My mother's parents, her brothers
and sisters

GRANDMOTHER   GRANDFATHER

married
(date)

_____
(maiden name)

b. _____
d. _____

_____
(name)

b. _____
d. _____

MY MOTHER, HER BROTHERS AND SISTERS

First born _____
    b. _____ d. _____
Marriage date _____
Spouse _____
    b. _____ d. _____
Children:
1. _____
    b. _____ d. _____
2. _____
    b. _____ d. _____

Second born _____
    b. _____ d. _____
Marriage date _____
Spouse _____
    b. _____ d. _____
Children:
1. _____
    b. _____ d. _____
2. _____
    b. _____ d. _____

Third born _____

      b._____ d._____

Marriage date _____

Spouse _____

      b. _____ d._____

Children:

1. _____

      b._____ d. _____

2. _____

      b._____ d._____

Fourth born _____

      b. _____ d._____

Marriage date _____

Spouse _____

      b._____ d._____

Children:

1. _____

      b. _____ d. _____

2. _____

      b. _____ d. _____

Other personal or historical data:

_____

_____

_____

_____

_____

_____

_____

_____

_____

GRANDMOTHER   GRANDFATHER

married
(date)

_____
(maiden name)

_____
(name)

b. _____

b. _____

d. _____

d. _____

MY FATHER, HIS BROTHERS
AND SISTERS

First born _____

      b. _____ d. _____

      Marriage date _____

      Spouse _____

      b. _____ d. _____

      Children:

      1. _____

      b. _____ d. _____

      2. _____

      b. _____ d. _____

Second born _____

      b. _____ d. _____

      Marriage date _____

      Spouse _____

      b. _____ d. _____

      Children:

      1. _____

      b. _____ d. _____

      2. _____

      b. _____ d. _____

Third born _____

     b._____ d. _____

    Marriage date _____

    Spouse _____

     b. _____ d. _____

    Children:

    1. _____

     b._____ d. _____

    2. _____

     b._____ d. _____

Fourth born _____

     b. _____ d. _____

    Marriage date _____

    Spouse _____

     b. _____ d. _____

    Children:

    1. _____

     b._____ d. _____

    2. _____

     b. _____ d. _____

Other personal or historical data:

_____

_____

_____

_____

_____

_____

_____

_____

_____

GREAT-GRANDMOTHER

GREAT-GRANDFATHER

married
(date)

_____
(maiden name)

b. _____
d. _____

_____
(name)

b. _____
d. _____

MY MATERNAL GRANDMOTHER, HER BROTHERS AND SISTERS

First born _____
    b. _____ d. _____
Marriage date _____
Spouse _____
    b. _____ d. _____
Children:
    1. _____
      b. _____ d. _____
    2. _____
      b. _____ d. _____

Second born _____
    b. _____ d. _____
Marriage date _____
Spouse _____
    b. _____ d. _____
Children:
    1. _____
      b. _____ d. _____
    2. _____
      b. _____ d. _____

Third born _____
      b._____ d. _____
Marriage date _____
Spouse _____
      b. _____ d. _____
Children:
    1. _____
      b._____ d. _____
    2. _____
      b. _____ d. _____

Fourth born _____
      b. _____ d. _____
Marriage date _____
Spouse _____
      b. _____ d. _____
Children:
    1. _____
      b. _____ d. _____
    2. _____
      b. _____ d. _____

Other personal or historical data:

_____
_____
_____
_____
_____
_____
_____
_____
_____

My mother's grandparents on her _____ 65
father's side

GREAT-
GRANDMOTHER

GREAT-
GRANDFATHER

married
(date)

_____
(maiden name)
b. _____
d. _____

_____
(name)
b. _____
d. _____

MY MATERNAL GRANDFATHER, HIS BROTHERS AND SISTERS

First born _____
    b. _____ d. _____
Marriage date _____
Spouse _____
    b. _____ d. _____
Children:
1. _____
    b. _____ d. _____
2. _____
    b. _____ d. _____

Second born _____
    b. _____ d. _____
Marriage date _____
Spouse _____
    b. _____ d. _____
Children:
1. _____
    b. _____ d. _____
2. _____
    b. _____ d. _____

Third born _____

     b. _____ d. _____

Marriage date _____

Spouse _____

     b. _____ d. _____

Children:

1. _____

     b. _____ d. _____

2. _____

     b. _____ d. _____

Fourth born _____

     b. _____ d. _____

Marriage date _____

Spouse _____

     b. _____ d. _____

Children:

1. _____

     b. _____ d. _____

2. _____

     b. _____ d. _____

Other personal or historical data:

_____

_____

_____

_____

_____

_____

_____

_____

_____

GREAT-GRANDMOTHER   GREAT-GRANDFATHER

married
(date)

———————————
(maiden name)

b. ———————————
d. ———————————

———————————
(name)

b. ———————————
d. ———————————

MY PATERNAL GRANDMOTHER, HER BROTHERS AND SISTERS

First born ——————————————————————
      b. ———————————— d. ——————————
Marriage date ———————————————————————
Spouse ——————————————————————————
      b. ———————————— d. ——————————
Children:
      1. ——————————————————————————
          b. ———————————— d. ——————————
      2. ——————————————————————————
          b. ———————————— d. ——————————

Second born ——————————————————————
      b. ———————————— d. ——————————
Marriage date ———————————————————————
Spouse ——————————————————————————
      b. ———————————— d. ——————————
Children:
      1. ——————————————————————————
          b. ———————————— d. ——————————
      2. ——————————————————————————
          b. ———————————— d. ——————————

Third born _____

     b._____ d._____

Marriage date _____

Spouse _____

     b. _____ d._____

Children:

1. _____

     b._____ d. _____

2. _____

     b._____ d. _____

Fourth born _____

     b. _____ d. _____

Marriage date _____

Spouse _____

     b._____ d. _____

Children:

1. _____

     b._____ d. _____

2. _____

     b. _____ d. _____

Other personal or historical data:

_____

_____

_____

_____

_____

_____

_____

_____

_____

GREAT-GRANDMOTHER

GREAT-GRANDFATHER

married
(date)

————————
(maiden name)

b. ————————
d. ————————

————————
(name)

b. ————————
d. ————————

MY PATERNAL GRANDFATHER, HIS BROTHERS AND SISTERS

First born ————————————————
      b. ———————— d. ————————
Marriage date ————————————————
Spouse ————————————————
      b. ———————— d. ————————
Children:
  1. ————————————————
      b. ———————— d. ————————
  2. ————————————————
      b. ———————— d. ————————

Second born ————————————————
      b. ———————— d. ————————
Marriage date ————————————————
Spouse ————————————————
      b. ———————— d. ————————
Children:
  1. ————————————————
      b. ———————— d. ————————
  2. ————————————————
      b. ———————— d. ————————

Third born _____
     b. _____ d. _____
    Marriage date _____
    Spouse _____
     b. _____ d. _____
    Children:
    1. _____
     b. _____ d. _____
    2. _____
     b. _____ d. _____

Fourth born _____
     b. _____ d. _____
    Marriage date _____
    Spouse _____
     b. _____ d. _____
    Children:
    1. _____
     b. _____ d. _____
    2. _____
     b. _____ d. _____

Other personal or historical data:

_____
_____
_____
_____
_____
_____
_____
_____
_____
_____

The other side of the family

(Family's name)

FOR
A
FAVORITE
PHOTO

SPOUSE   ME

(write full name)   _(write full name)_

married
(date)

b._____   b._____
d._____   d._____

MY CHILDREN AND GRANDCHILDREN

First born _____
    b. _____ d. _____
Marriage date _____
Spouse _____
    b. _____ d. _____
Children:
1. _____
    b. _____ d. _____
2. _____
    b. _____ d. _____

Second born _____
    b. _____ d. _____
Marriage date _____
Spouse _____
    b. _____ d. _____
Children:
1. _____
    b. _____ d. _____
2. _____
    b. _____ d. _____

Third born _____
    b. _____ d. _____
    Child's marriage date _____
    Child's spouse _____
    b. _____ d. _____
Third born's children:
    1. _____
       b. _____ d. _____
    2. _____
       b. _____ d. _____

Other personal or historical data which you
may want to note. You can include educational accomplishments, trades and professions,
other important dates, burial sites, remarriages,
places of birth:

_____

_____

_____

_____

_____

_____

_____

_____

_____

_____

_____

_____

_____

_____

My other marriages:
  To whom _____
       b. _____ d. _____
  Marriage years _____
Children of marriage:
First born _____
       b. _____ d. _____
  Child's marriage date _____
  Child's spouse _____
       b. _____ d. _____
First born's children:
  1. _____
       b. _____ d. _____
  2. _____
       b. _____ d. _____
Second born _____
       b. _____ d. _____
  Child's marriage date _____
  Child's spouse _____
       b. _____ d. _____
Second born's children:
  1. _____
       b. _____ d. _____
  2. _____
       b. _____ d. _____

Other personal or historical data:

_____
_____
_____
_____
_____
_____

Spouse's other marriages:
   To whom _____
       b. _____ d. _____
   Marriage years _____
Children of marriage:
First born _____
       b. _____ d. _____
   Child's marriage date _____
   Child's spouse _____
       b. _____ d. _____
First born's children:
   1. _____
       b. _____ d. _____
   2. _____
       b. _____ d. _____
Second born _____
       b. _____ d. _____
   Child's marriage date _____
   Child's spouse _____
       b. _____ d. _____
Second born's children:
   1. _____
       b. _____ d. _____
   2. _____
       b. _____ d. _____

Other personal or historical data:

_____
_____
_____
_____
_____
_____

MOTHER   FATHER

married
(date)

_____
(maiden name)

b._____
d._____

_____
(name)

b._____
d._____

ME, MY BROTHERS AND SISTERS

First born _____
    b. _____ d. _____
Marriage date _____
Spouse _____
    b. _____ d. _____
Children:
    1. _____
        b. _____ d. _____
    2. _____
        b. _____ d. _____

Second born _____
    b. _____ d. _____
Marriage date _____
Spouse _____
    b. _____ d. _____
Children:
    1. _____
        b. _____ d. _____
    2. _____
        b. _____ d. _____

Third born _____

     b._____ d. _____

Marriage date _____

Spouse _____

     b. _____ d. _____

Children:

1. _____

     b._____ d. _____

2. _____

     b._____ d. _____

Fourth born _____

     b. _____ d. _____

Marriage date _____

Spouse _____

     b._____ d. _____

Children:

1. _____

     b._____ d. _____

2. _____

     b. _____ d. _____

Other personal or historical data:

_____

_____

_____

_____

_____

_____

_____

_____

_____

GRANDMOTHER   GRANDFATHER

married
(date)

_____
(maiden name)

b._____
d._____

_____
(name)

b._____
d._____

MY MOTHER, HER BROTHERS
AND SISTERS

First born _____

    b. _____ d. _____

Marriage date _____

Spouse _____

    b. _____ d. _____

Children:

1. _____

    b. _____ d. _____

2. _____

    b. _____ d. _____

Second born _____

    b._____ d. _____

Marriage date _____

Spouse _____

    b. _____ d. _____

Children:

1. _____

    b._____ d. _____

2. _____

    b._____ d. _____

Third born _____

     b._____ d._____

     Marriage date _____

     Spouse_____

     b._____ d._____

     Children:

     1. _____

        b._____ d._____

     2. _____

        b._____ d._____

Fourth born _____

     b._____ d._____

     Marriage date _____

     Spouse_____

     b._____ d._____

     Children:

     1. _____

        b._____ d._____

     2. _____

        b._____ d._____

Other personal or historical data:

_____

_____

_____

_____

_____

_____

_____

_____

_____

GRANDMOTHER   GRANDFATHER

married
(date)

_____
(maiden name)

b. _____
d. _____

_____
(name)

b. _____
d. _____

MY FATHER, HIS BROTHERS
AND SISTERS

First born _____
    b. _____ d. _____
Marriage date _____
Spouse _____
    b. _____ d. _____
Children:
  1. _____
    b. _____ d. _____
  2. _____
    b. _____ d. _____

Second born _____
    b. _____ d. _____
Marriage date _____
Spouse _____
    b. _____ d. _____
Children:
  1. _____
    b. _____ d. _____
  2. _____
    b. _____ d. _____

Third born _____

     b._____ d. _____

Marriage date _____

Spouse _____

     b. _____ d. _____

Children:

1. _____

     b._____ d. _____

2. _____

     b._____ d. _____

Fourth born _____

     b. _____ d. _____

Marriage date _____

Spouse _____

     b. _____ d. _____

Children:

1. _____

     b. _____ d. _____

2. _____

     b. _____ d. _____

Other personal or historical data:

_____

_____

_____

_____

_____

_____

_____

_____

_____

_____

GREAT-GRANDMOTHER

GREAT-GRANDFATHER

married
(date)

_____
(maiden name)

b. _____
d. _____

_____
(name)

b. _____
d. _____

MY MATERNAL GRANDMOTHER, HER BROTHERS AND SISTERS

First born _____
    b. _____ d. _____
Marriage date _____
Spouse _____
    b. _____ d. _____
Children:
1. _____
    b. _____ d. _____
2. _____
    b. _____ d. _____

Second born _____
    b. _____ d. _____
Marriage date _____
Spouse _____
    b. _____ d. _____
Children:
1. _____
    b. _____ d. _____
2. _____
    b. _____ d. _____

Third born _____
     b._____ d. _____
     Marriage date _____
     Spouse_____
     b. _____ d. _____
     Children:
     1. _____
        b._____ d. _____
     2. _____
        b. _____ d. _____

Fourth born _____
     b. _____ d. _____
     Marriage date _____
     Spouse _____
     b._____ d. _____
     Children:
     1. _____
        b. _____ d. _____
     2. _____
        b. _____ d. _____

Other personal or historical data:

_____
_____
_____
_____
_____
_____
_____
_____
_____
_____

GREAT-
GRANDMOTHER

GREAT-
GRANDFATHER

married
(date)

_____
(maiden name)

b. _____

d. _____

_____
(name)

b. _____

d. _____

MY MATERNAL GRANDFATHER, HIS BROTHERS AND SISTERS

First born _____

    b. _____ d. _____

    Marriage date _____

    Spouse _____

    b. _____ d. _____

    Children:

    1. _____

    b. _____ d. _____

    2. _____

    b. _____ d. _____

Second born _____

    b. _____ d. _____

    Marriage date _____

    Spouse _____

    b. _____ d. _____

    Children:

    1. _____

    b. _____ d. _____

    2. _____

    b. _____ d. _____

Third born _____

    b._____ d. _____

Marriage date _____

Spouse _____

    b. _____ d. _____

Children:

1. _____

    b._____ d. _____

2. _____

    b._____ d. _____

Fourth born _____

    b. _____ d. _____

Marriage date _____

Spouse _____

    b._____ d. _____

Children:

1. _____

    b. _____ d. _____

2. _____

    b. _____ d. _____

Other personal or historical data:

_____

_____

_____

_____

_____

_____

_____

_____

_____

_____

GREAT-GRANDMOTHER

GREAT-GRANDFATHER

married
(date)

_____
(maiden name)

b. _____
d. _____

_____
(name)

b. _____
d. _____

MY PATERNAL GRANDMOTHER, HER BROTHERS AND SISTERS

First born _____
    b. _____ d. _____
Marriage date _____
Spouse _____
    b. _____ d. _____
Children:
    1. _____
      b. _____ d. _____
    2. _____
      b. _____ d. _____

Second born _____
    b. _____ d. _____
Marriage date _____
Spouse _____
    b. _____ d. _____
Children:
    1. _____
      b. _____ d. _____
    2. _____
      b. _____ d. _____

Third born _____

     b._____ d. _____

    Marriage date _____

    Spouse _____

      b. _____ d. _____

    Children:

    1. _____

      b._____ d. _____

    2. _____

      b. _____ d. _____

Fourth born _____

     b. _____ d. _____

    Marriage date _____

    Spouse _____

      b. _____ d. _____

    Children:

    1. _____

      b. _____ d. _____

    2. _____

      b. _____ d. _____

Other personal or historical data:

_____

_____

_____

_____

_____

_____

_____

_____

_____

GREAT-
GRANDMOTHER

GREAT-
GRANDFATHER

married
(date)

_____
(maiden name)

b. _____

d. _____

_____
(name)

b. _____

d. _____

MY PATERNAL GRANDFATHER, HIS BROTHERS AND SISTERS

First born _____

    b. _____ d. _____

    Marriage date _____

    Spouse _____

    b. _____ d. _____

    Children:

    1. _____

      b. _____ d. _____

    2. _____

      b. _____ d. _____

Second born _____

    b. _____ d. _____

    Marriage date _____

    Spouse _____

    b. _____ d. _____

    Children:

    1. _____

      b. _____ d. _____

    2. _____

      b. _____ d. _____

Third born _____

      b. _____ d. _____

Marriage date _____

Spouse _____

      b. _____ d. _____

Children:

1. _____

      b. _____ d. _____

2. _____

      b. _____ d. _____

Fourth born _____

      b. _____ d. _____

Marriage date _____

Spouse _____

      b. _____ d. _____

Children:

1. _____

      b. _____ d. _____

2. _____

      b. _____ d. _____

Other personal or historical data:

_____

_____

_____

_____

_____

_____

_____

_____

_____

LEARNING BY ASKING
A Guide for Educators

For some time now I have been encouraging and helping educators teach young people of all ages how to become family or neighborhood journalists and interview their close relatives and friends.

The tape recorder enables us to capture these stories on tape and create new kinds of home, school or classroom reference libraries of spoken history, or *Instant Oral Biographies*. We can go there and play cassettes to help us answer the questions we have about life the same way we play tapes of music. Videotape recorders and film cameras, if available, can be used, too.

Educators and parents find having young people interview others for their life stories is an excellent way to learn about history, social studies, cultural differences and journalism. The answers and new perspectives gained from interviewing people of different backgrounds help all of us little by little fill in the mosaic of what it means to live in this world.

Moreover, conducting an interview certainly enhances language, listening and memory skills and helps instill even greater self-confidence in young people, particularly shy ones or those with speech problems. It provides a structure that propels them to reach out to another person.

Let us also not minimize the value of interviews as tools to awaken empathy and sensitivity to others, and appreciation of good journalistic skills.

I encourage schools to use oral history interviews as focal points for "Grandparents Day" activities in which relatives, foster parents or close family friends are invited to school to spend time with the children and be questioned about their experiences.

The children take turns in interviewing as well as in "sharing" the relatives and friends who come, since there are never enough around. Similar activities linking the generations can be held at senior citizen centers and hospital nursing homes.

Some nursing homes, in fact, have begun programs involving local schools and colleges and volunteers to help their residents overcome their estrangement from the community at large. They are aware that older people are a prime source for first-hand historical knowledge about their communities; and, students who interview these people can preserve important pieces of local history that otherwise would be lost to future generations.

There is an African saying to the effect that when an old person dies, an entire library is destroyed. We must remember this.

Creative teachers can build exciting teaching units around taping or filming such interviews.

For example, for history, if a class is studying the subject of immigration, class visitors could be asked why and how they came to this country, what life was like for them at first, and how it differed from their country of birth.

The children, too, might be encouraged to draw family trees as an introduction to genealogical research.

If a class is studying another important historic period, such as the Great Depression, visitors could be asked for first-hand information about how they survived this harsh time and how their lives changed.

A teacher creating a social studies unit about cultural differences could encourage students to interview relatives to tape recipes for special foods cooked during holidays, or ask about customs associated with these special holidays.

For civics, the *Instant Oral Biography* interviewing techniques also can be used to encourage children to visit people in the community, to ask them about their jobs, or how the town or neighborhood has changed during the years.

Research teams can be assigned to certain projects—one to interview people who work in government, another to interview entrepreneurs, one to interview scientists, another to question artists.

The children could ask these people how they chose their professions, what they like or dislike about them, how they prepared for them and how they keep developing.

Or, how about an assignment called "Lessons from Life," where children interview adults about what it's like to be a parent, or what grownups were like when they were the children's age, what they were afraid of at that age, what they did to overcome a big problem, or what special things they learned that they are proud of.

We learn from such tapes that people of all backgrounds often share similar fears and feelings; in other instances we find people approach the same problems in different ways because of their own individual and cultural differences.

We also find there usually is no simple answer to an interviewer's question, that more often than not shades of gray predominate over black or white. And that we each have pieces of the full answer.

This is particularly evident when a child interviews two people in the same family and each gives a different version of the same story or incident—but from their special perspective. This is a journalist's first lesson.

Completed tapes become new reference tools. Some schools in fact are using them to initiate oral history libraries where children can come to play a tape of someone's life for reference or for pleasure in the same way they come to borrow a book.

Teachers also might want to encourage youngsters to take notes while interviewing even though a tape recorder is being used. Not only does such note-taking prove useful if a recorder fails, but note-taking often helps us listen more carefully and reinforces certain points made.

I would encourage children to form their own questions so that any interview is more meaningful to what they are interested in. These questions can be written on cards, with the specific questions selected for a child on the basis of his or her ability to read and articulate them.

Questions can, of course, be selected by the children from those listed in this book. I have found from working with very young people that they are most interested in asking older people for stories about the way they were when they were the children's age. For that reason, here are some very basic questions that could be used for a class taping:

■ What is your full name? And do you know what your name means? In what language?

■ When were you born? And where were you born?

■ When did your family first come to this country and where did they come from? Did they ever tell you what life was like for them before they came here? What did they bring with them?

■ What are your earliest memories of when you were a child?

■ What was your life like when you were my age? What did you do with your time when you were very young—go to school or work? Where did you live? What games did you play?

■ Can you tell me any stories to show me the way you were when you were very young?

■ What do you think is the most important thing that ever happened to you in your life? What was your greatest adventure?

■ Do you remember any especially funny or sad stories about your life?

■ What special things do you know that you are proud of?

■ Are there favorite family stories or sayings or songs that you can tell me? What are they? Can you tell them in a different language? Can you translate them for me? Are there family superstitions?

■ What things do you enjoy doing the most?

I emphasize these are just sample questions; the best ones would be those made up by the children themselves and which reflect what they want to learn from their elders.

It would be good to tell the youngsters that the answers they get will often raise even more questions about a subject, and that they should feel free enough to follow up on a question before starting a new subject. Thinking quickly and improvising new questions to reflect the turn of a conversation are something that all good journalists do. It is important that children be encouraged to listen carefully to the conversation and follow its course, rather than just go through the interview by rote, ticking off one prepared question after another.

Class visitors should be asked to bring family documents, scrapbooks, passports, birth, naturalization and marriage papers, old photographs and maps to show where they came from or once lived. They also can be encouraged to wear native dress of those countries where they were born or to bring handcrafts from these places.

And if you know in advance which relatives are coming, why not have the children research the countries of origin, their history and culture so that they can ask more informed questions?

Before a class taping is held, it would be useful for the children to practice asking the questions, whether by interviewing each other or their parents at home. In this way they are more comfortable when the actual interviewing takes place.

Also, it has been my experience that when a number of grandparents come to school, it is best to ask each to work with a group of four to six children; this allows every youngster to ask at least a question or two. Also, conduct the interviews one at a time so that other children in the class benefit from hearing the stories and observing the interview process. One interview at a time also helps keep the sound level down in a class; it makes for poor taping to have many interviews conducted simultaneously.

Youngsters also should be encouraged to write or phone requests for interviews and offer follow up thank-yous.

And, to reinforce what the children have learned and to improve reading, writing and editing skills, teachers also might want to consider encouraging youngsters to transcribe the tapes and bind the pages in book form.

We always learn something new in hearing or reading a story for a second time. Again, while making the tape or after rehearing it, you could have the interviewers write a summary sheet of the subjects covered and where on the tape they are found. Use the counter on the recorder for this purpose. How about including a glossary of unfamiliar expressions or words in another language?

These transcriptions can also provide the raw material for writing scripts for radio or video programs that a class might want to present to the rest of the school or to parents.

As for obtaining enough recording equipment to go around the class, it has been my experience from organizing such projects that many parents are only too glad to lend tape recorders to a class when they are informed by note of what a teacher is trying to accomplish.

Encourage the parents to have the children practice interviewing with them and help their children gather old family photographs or documents that could be used in the oral biographies.

And how about inviting the school or local newspaper to cover this important event?

Educators also might encourage children to interview each other and share experiences. For example, the interviews might be focused on a theme such as: "My Strangest Experience"; "How I Can Become More Powerful"; "If I Had Three Wishes"; "The Things I Know Best"; "My Saddest Memory"; "The Happiest Day in My Life"; "My Biggest Fear and How I Try to Overcome It."

And to help stimulate their own creativity, why not consider having the children answer questions in a language they make up by themselves and write an accompanying dictionary to help others understand what they are saying.

Finally, for language teachers, the interviews also provide good practice for those trying to speak or understand another language. For practice you might want to ask the questions in the language of the person you interview, with that person answering you in your own language. Such interviews also help prepare one who has difficulties with language to communicate more effectively for real life experiences, such as applying for a job or to school. Interviewing is a perfect activity for speech therapy, too.

One of the greatest benefits derived from encouraging individuals to become interviewers is that they are drawn closer to other people just by the process of having to interact with someone through a question-answer format.

This process can be undertaken not only by normal children, but by exceptional ones who may be blind, learning impaired, retarded, and who suffer from other physical and emotional handicaps.

Teachers and parents can modify the oral biography interview procedures for the particular needs of such children. This may mean, for example, having a youngster ask only one question of someone in order to insure that he or she can make the achievement of obtaining an appropriate answer or story. Being able to ask a question, obtain an answer and hear both on tape can go far to enhance a child's self-image.

Children with handicaps know what it is to face and overcome rejection by others who fear or do not understand them. But, with the interaction that comes from good interviewing, not only can these youngsters learn to communicate more effectively with others, but they can overcome in part other people's fear of their differences.

Good interviewing helps to enhance the self-image of all people—normal and exceptional.

"What's your happiest memory?"

William Zimmerman, the creator of *HOW TO TAPE INSTANT ORAL BIOGRAPHIES,* has been a questioner all his life. A journalist for more than 25 years, Mr. Zimmerman is special projects editor of Newsday, the daily newspaper. His other books are: *A BOOK OF QUESTIONS to keep thoughts and feelings,* a new form of diary/journal; *MAKE BELIEFS,* a gift book for the imagination that readers can complete with pencil, crayon, or paintbrush, and *LIFELINES: A Book of Hope,* which offers comforting thoughts to help people get through difficult times in life.

Guarionex Press (pronounced Gwah-ree-oh-nex) was named after a proud Taino Indian chief who lived in Puerto Rico in the sixteenth century. He fought bravely and fiercely against the Spanish, leading the last major Indian insurrection against the war-hardened, better-armed Spanish Army. When Zimmerman and his wife, who is Puerto Rican, decided to start their kitchen-table press in 1979, they knew they too, would have to be brave in order to survive as a small business and named their press Guarionex.

Books that affirm the power of
the imagination and human spirit
to overcome life's problems.

 **Guarionex Press Ltd.**

Gifts for your imagination from Guarionex Press

HOW TO TAPE INSTANT ORAL BIOGRAPHIES
by William Zimmerman

Step by step, a journalist shows you and your family how to tape record, videotape or film your life stories, memories and traditions. Offers basic interviewing techniques, questions to ask, 35 blank family history sheets, and teacher's guide.
112 pages with photos, $8.95 each by mail order (including postage) from Guarionex Press or $6.95 in stores. ISBN 0-935966-00-5, 6"x 9", for all ages.

MAKE BELIEFS: A Gift for Your Imagination
by Bill Zimmerman
drawings by Tom Bloom

This coloring playbook helps you see the world differently—with help from a special question-answer format that encourages you to imagine, and which you complete with crayon, pencil or paintbrush.
96 pages with over 70 drawings, $8.95 each by mail order (including postage) from Guarionex Press or $6.95 in stores. ISBN 0-935966-03-X, 6"x 9", for all ages.

A BOOK OF QUESTIONS to keep thoughts and feelings
by William Zimmerman

For those who want help in keeping a diary/journal. By writing your answers to the book's provocative questions, you create your own Journal of Thoughts. Tiny enough to fit in your pocket.
256 pages, $7.95 each by mail order (including postage) or $5.95 in stores. ISBN 0-935966-01-3, 3"x 5¼", for all age groups.

LIFELINES: A Book of Hope
by Bill Zimmerman
drawings by Tom Bloom

Comforting thoughts to get you through life's hard times with humor and spirit. Offers gentle good advice in the form of 59 "life lines" that cover situations from losing someone you love, to recovering from an illness or broken heart, to coping with an angry teenager.
128 pages with more than 100 drawings, $8.95 each by mail order (including postage) or $6.95 in stores. ISBN 0-935966-04-8, 6"x 6½", for all ages.

To order by mail send check to:
Guarionex Press Ltd., Attn: William Zimmerman
201 West 77th Street, New York, NY 10024 To order by phone call 1-212-724-5259
Please give your name and address and that of the person you wish to receive the gift book.
Special price for all four books $31.00.